Ontario Breeze

by Phebe White

Henderson, New York
Jefferson County

January 1, 1869 - September 19, 1869

transcribed by Diane Janowski

New York History Review Press
Elmira, New York

Ontario Breeze

by Phebe White
transcribed by Diane Janowski
Copyright © 2012 New York History Review Press

Published by New York History Review Press
Elmira, New York

Notice of Rights. All rights reserved. No part of this book may be reproduced or transmitted in any form by any means, electronic, mechanical, photocopying, recording or otherwise, without the prior written permission of the author. For more information on getting permission for reprints and excerpts, contact us through our website.
www.NewYorkHistoryReview.com

For the latest on New York History Review, please visit
www.NewYorkHistoryReview.com

ISBN: 978-0-9838487-3-8

First Edition

Printed in the United States of America

Cover image: Summer home of Mrs. B. R. Stillman, Henderson, New York. Courtesy of the Eleanor Barnes Library.

1869 March 27

*In three years from today
where will Jule White, Flora White,
Phebe White & Mate Boyce be?*

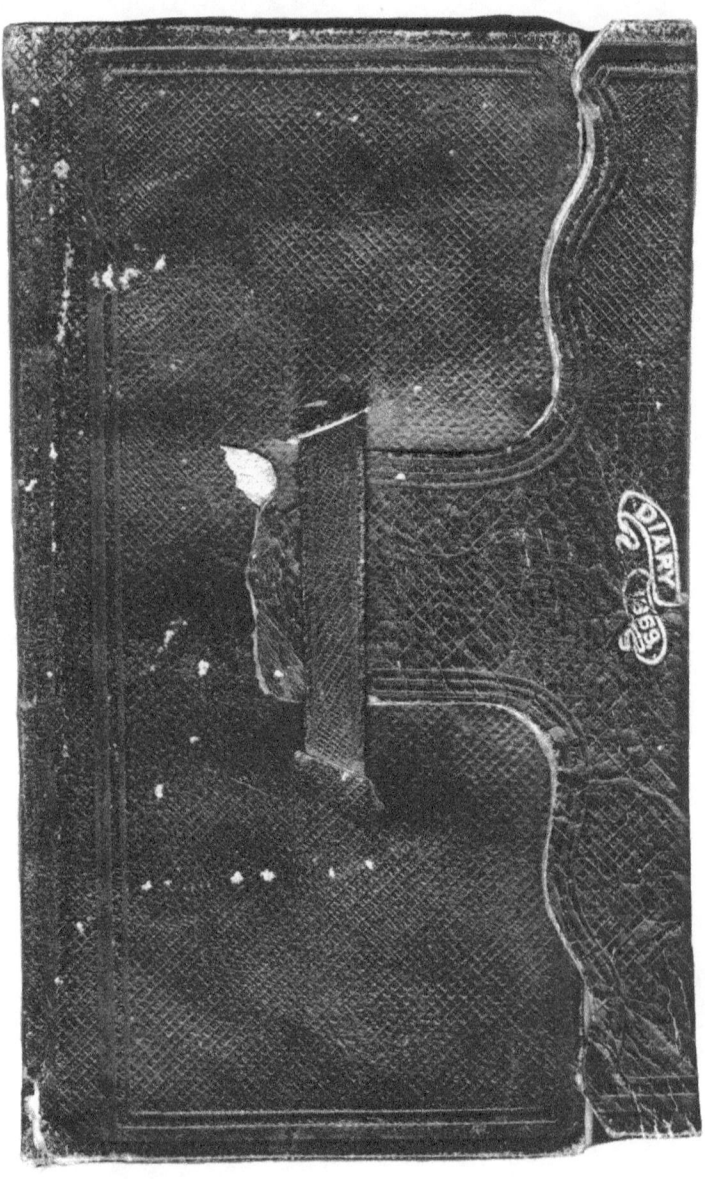

Phebe's diary in its current condition.
Courtesy of the Eleanor Barnes Library, Elmira, New York.

Table of Contents

Foreward..8
Maps of Henderson, New York........................10, 11
People in the Diary..12
Ontario Breeze 19
Afterward..77
Bibiliography..78

Foreward

In our *Learning from History* series of Upstate New York diaries, accounts of young people's lives on the farm, or in the home, help us to understand their thoughts and experiences. Each narrative offers a unique perspective on young peoples' lives in rural New York, and serves as an important primary resource in the study of American history.

Ontario Breeze is the journal of 18-year-old Phebe White of Henderson, New York in Jefferson County.

Phebe was born around 1851 in Henderson, the daughter of James and Hannah White. Her father was a ship builder. She had a recently-married older sister Julia, called "Jule," and younger sister Jennie, age 12. Also Phebe had two younger brothers, Albert, age 13, a sailor on Lake Ontario, and Everett, age 10. Jule often stayed at her parents' house while her husband Mont was away sailing.

Beginning on January 1, 1869, Phebe recorded the events of her life in a small 3 x 6 inch pocket diary with three entries to the page in very nice handwriting. Phebe's notations were confined to the spaces allotted and are written in ink. Her handwriting is mostly legible, except for a few names or places that cannot be deciphered. Phebe's spelling is left as she spelled it. Clarifications have been added in brackets. The photographed pages from his diary are actual size.

Phebe lived with her parents. She had plenty of friends, boyfriends, and neighbors. She was generally very happy in her life – she enjoyed her family and friends. Phebe was finishing her last year of school in 1869.

Ontario Breeze invites us into the daily life of a New York young woman through her own words and experiences. We hear Phebe's voice as she shares her joys, sorrows, enthusiasm, and fragility of life in a rural ship-building community.

The Eleanor Barnes Library acquired Phebe White's diary in 2011. So far as is known, this transcription is its first published version.

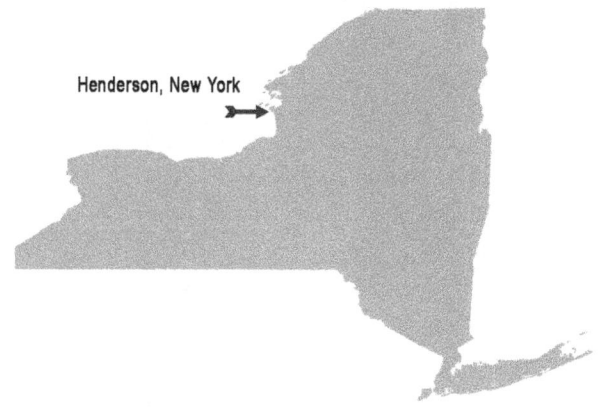

View of Henderson Harbor from the Gill House. Published by Beach's Photography, circa 1890.

SIX TOWN POINT
HENDERSON BAY
HENDERSON HARBOR
HENDERSON P.O
Henderson Pond
Stony Creek

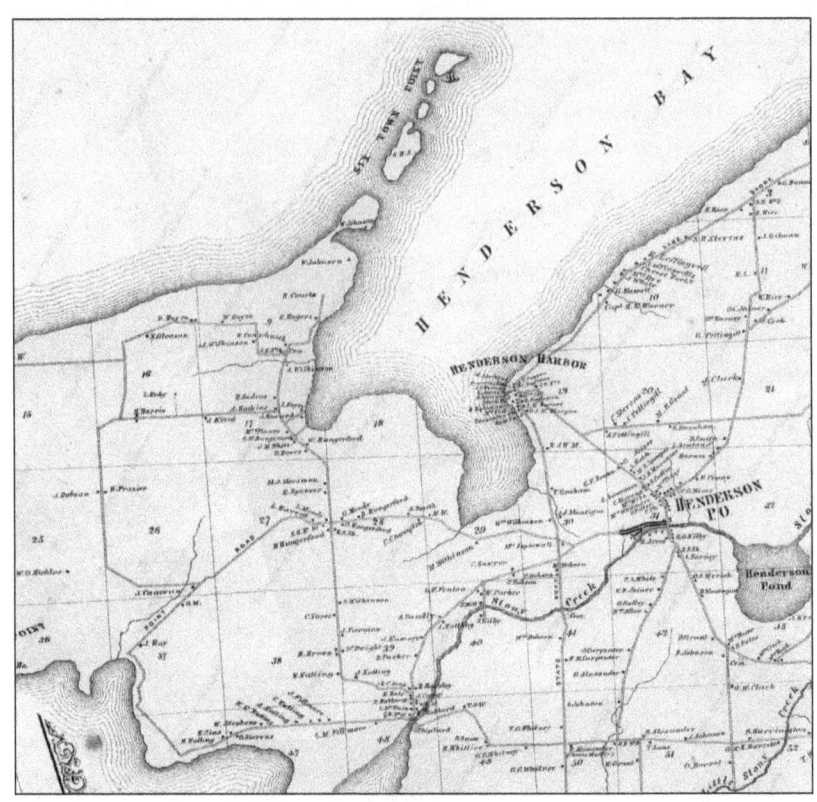

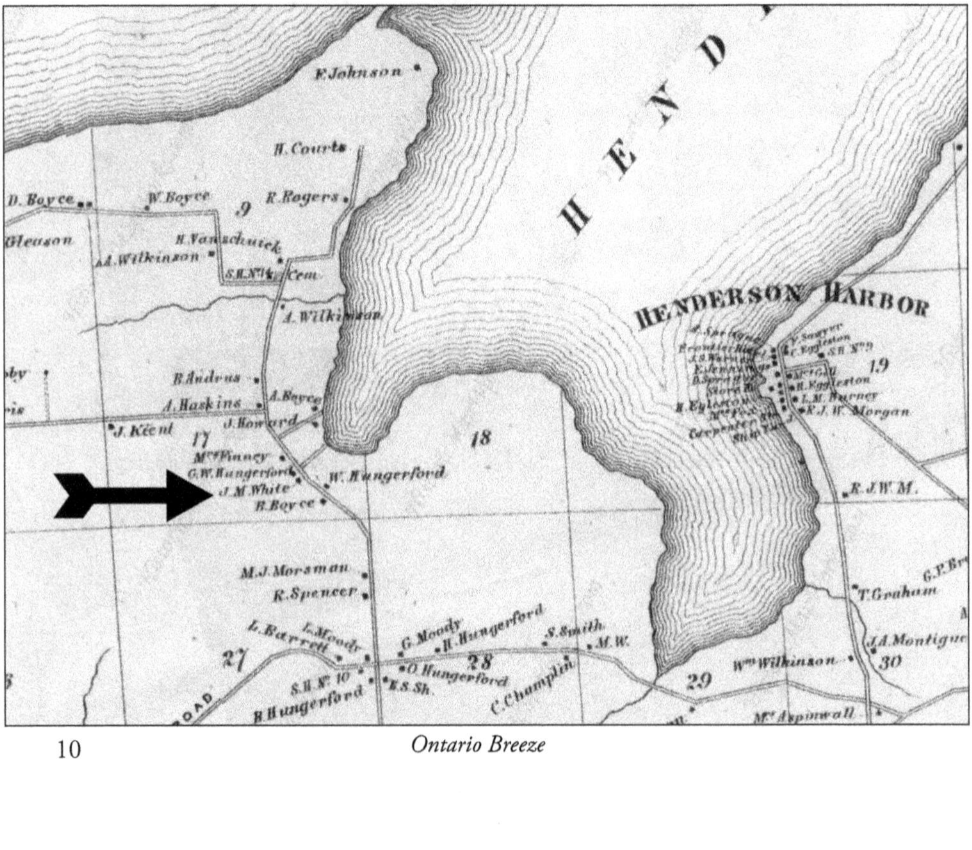
F. Johnson
H. Courts
D. Boyce
W. Boyce
R. Rogers
9
Gleason
H. Vanschuick
A. Wilkinson
S.H. No. 11
Cem.
A. Wilkinson
HEND
HENDERSON HARBOR
B. Andrus
A. Haskins
A. Boyce
J. Keenl
J. Howard
17
18
Mc Finney
G.W. Hungerford
W. Hungerford
J.M. White
B. Boyce
19
L.M. Warner
R.J.W.M.
M.J. Morsman
R. Spencer
T. Graham
L. Barrett
L. Moody
G. Moody
H. Hungerford
S. Smith
M.W.
27
28
S.H. No. 10
O. Hungerford
E.S. Sh.
B. Hungerford
C. Champlin
29
Wm Wilkinson
J.A. Montigue
30
Mr. Aspinwall

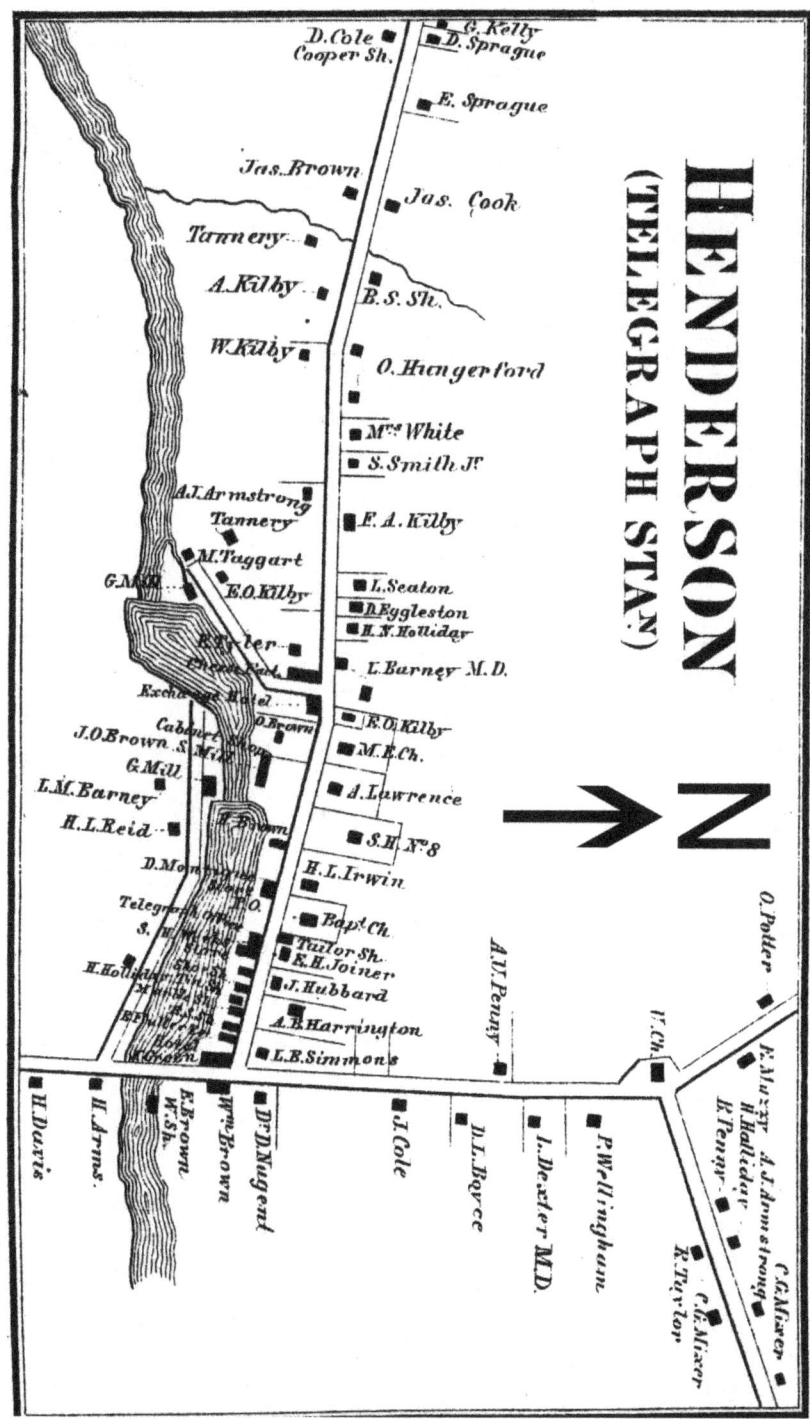

Maps of Henderson, New York and surrounding areas. *Jefferson County Gazetteer 1864* by C. K. Stone. On the opposite page, the arrow shows Phebe's home.

People in the diary
Phebe's family

James White - father, age 50
Hannah White - mother, age 48
Jule - older sister Julia Sprague - age 21- married to Almont [Mont] a sailor who was frequently away
Albert - younger brother - age 13, sailor on Lake Ontario
Everett - younger brother - age 10
Jennie - younger sister, age 12
Aunt Julia [Hungerford] age 48 & Uncle Washington, sailor, age 54 - lived across the street
Aunt Susan
Aunt Mary Vorce
Uncle Ed & Aunt Eliza
Uncle William Wilkinson
Uncle Richard & Builda

Family and Friends

Abigail
Addie & Charlie
Barney
Katie Barrett
Ell Bartlett
Herb Bartlett
Belle
Mr. Borden & Connelly
Mate Boyce
Leslie Boyce - sailor, age 19
Elvira Boyce - age 40 - married to Birdsall, lived next door
Birdsall Boyce - age 46, farmer
Wat Boyce
Orlando Bright [Albright?]
Mrs. Bullfinch
Mrs. Burnham
Byron
Ernie C

Doctor Chapman
Cranage
Em Crowell
Simeon Danley
Delia & Francis
Peter Demell - farmer with raspberries - age 51
Mary Dings [spelled Dnigs in 1870 census] age 18 - married to Martin in Henderson
Aunt Dork [Dorcas] age 46, Uncle Charles Eggleston - sailor - age 48
Addie Eggleston - cousin, age 19 (daughter of Dorcas and Charles)
Frank Dobson
Eva & Hollie
Ellen
Charles Ellis
C.R. Ellis
Joe Finney
George
Olive Gill
Delia Gleason [Adelia, Deal] - age 18
Laura Gleason - age 39, married to Nathanial
Miles Gleason - farmer, age 25
Victoria Gleason - music teacher, age 30 - lived with the Joiner family in Henderson
Earl Green
Mert H
Harry
Hen [Henry] Houghton - age 20
Dolla Halliday - age 16
Mort Halliday
Hine - maybe Hind
Everett Hollis
Hovey
Howard
Charlie Howard
C.D. Howard
Delia Howard
Ell Howard
Harlie Howard

Albert Hungerford
Aunt Susan [Hungerford]
Ellie or Ebbie Jeff
Jensen
Jim
Frank K
Arthur K[Kilby] - store clerk, age 21
David Kilby
Mrs. Ebbie [Caroline] Kilby - age 41
Charlie Little
Jennie Lovell
Mrs. Luce
Marion
Melvin & Eve
Millie - had a fight with her
Charlie Mines
Mines or Miner
David Montague
Lewis Marin [Marron]
Mrs. Howard Martin
Charlie Mines
Moody
Myron & Jennie
Nettie
Noah
Anna Nugent
Orin
Charles Partridge - boyfriend [eventually husband] age 21 - born in Michigan - spelled "Patridge" in 1860 census
Peter
Mrs. Ray
Myron Ray
Rosette
Shellie [Charles] Rounds - age 15 - distant cousin lived with Uncle Bill Wilkinson
Marie S
Jim Seaton
Simmons

Brate [Braton] Snow - farmer, age 23
Em [Emma] Snow - age 18
Clara Sprague - age 15
Eliza Sprague - daughter of Dorcas and Charles, age 20
Jeddie Sprage
Mont [Almont] Sprague - husband of sister Jule, sailor, age 23
Bill Taylor
Fanny Thompson
Vandyne [Orange Vandyne] - married to Lucy, age 28
Leslie Vandyne
Wesley Vandyne
Lucy Vandyne - age 22, lived next door
Ell [Ellen] Vorce - age 16
Nick Vorce
Sophia Vorce - age 32
Myron W
Walker
Addie Walker
Warner - probably John Warner, hotel keeper, age 64
Mr. Washburn
Albert White
Florence White
Ell [Ella] Whitney - age 19 - lived in Henderson
Frank Whitney - brother of Ella, age 21
Wortley [or Worthley] Whitney - farm laborer - age 18 - lived in Henderson
Rosette Wilkinson - age 24 lived in Henderson - married to Albert Wilkinson
Carrie Worthingham - teacher

The business of the village of Henderson is as follows:

Mrs. H. D. Geeson, postmistress.

Payson F. Thompson, dry goods, boots and shoes; also telephone office.

The Hough Sisters, millinery.

Hungerford & Barthel, general store.

Charles D. Irwin, harness maker.

F. M. Kilby, drugs, general merchandise.

F. A. Kilby, shoe maker.

Frank Hadcock, proprietor of Eureka grist-mill.

David Hunter, blacksmith.

Dr. W. G. Terry, physician and surgeon.

Edward Everson, meat market.

M. C. McKee, blacksmith.

E. C. Sawyer, general merchandise.

Ira Ives, boot and shoe store.

W. H. Cross, blacksmith.

A. N. Leffiingwell, attorney and counsellor.

The Windsor House, S. E. & J. D. Wheeler, proprietors.

Dr. O. F. Buell, physician and surgeon.

W. E. Boyce, druggist and jeweller.

The Phelps House, H. H. Gill, proprietor.

The Henderson cheese factory, established in 1864, Emory Fales, proprietor; Benjamin Worthingham, maker.

Daniel B. Nugent, physician and surgeon.

From *The growth of a century: as illustrated in the history of Jefferson County, New York, from 1793-1894* by John A. Haddock., page 576.

From *History of Jefferson County, New York,* 1878 page 378A.

Names of ships that were of importance to Phebe. Written on the inside of the diary.

Phebe White
Henderson
Jefferson County, New York

January, Friday 1, 1869
Rained all day. Stayed at home. Went over to Aunt Julia's - stayed to supper. [in pencil] & I guess I stayed in the evening.

January, Saturday 2, 1869
Pleasant. Stayed at home all day. Mate over here.

January, Sunday 3, 1869
Pleasant in the morning, but rained before night. Went down to see Jule [older sister]. Brate [Braton Snow] & Ell was there. Hen Houghton & Ellie Jeff came down. I was not at home. Went down to Uncle Ed's. Florence came as far as Aunt Julia's with me. Charlie Little was there to see Mate.

January, Monday 4, 1869
Pleasant - went to school. Mate was over here this eve.

January, Tuesday 5, 1869
Pleasant - went to the school. Went to the lodge in the eve. Went to the Hallidays to a dance. Had fun all but Mont & Ebbie Jeff had a fight. Went with Wort Whitney. Got home at 5 o'clock. Mate stopped in.

January, Wednesday 6, 1869
Pleasant. Went to school. Rather sleepy. Went to a spelling school at night. Stayed till recess then went over to Lewis Marin [Marron]. Charlie, Jim, Jule, Harlie, Leslie, Arthur and I stayed [til] 10 o'clock.

January, Thursday 7, 1869
Pleasant - went to school - had an invite to go down to Hoveys to a party. Did not accept.

January, Friday 8, 1869
Pleasant - went to school part of the day. Charlie came up after Mate & I. Addie & Aunt Dork [Dorcas] Uncle Charles [Eggleston] was to Aunt Julia's. We started for the school house to go to meeting. Heard there was none. Went to Howard's and stayed a few minutes. Harlie came home with us.

January, Saturday 9, 1869
Raining as hard as it can possible. Was intending to go over to the Harbor but could not. Jule's birthday.

January, Sunday 10, 1869
Pleasant. Went down on the ice. Saw Henry H, Mert H, Harlie H, & Leslie, Mont, Jim. Went down again in the eve. Stayed till seven o'clock then Charlie H came home with me & stayed the eve. Went down to see Jule. Devil of a time. Jim down there.

January, Monday 11, 1869
Pleasant in the morning. Went over to the Harts to see the horses trot. Snowed good enough to spoil the skating. Saw Charlie, Jim, Ernie, Harlie, Leslie, Hen Houghton. Jim's drunk as a fool.

January, Tuesday 12, 1869
Snowing and blowing. Did not go to school. Eased off before night. Went to the Lodge. Came home at -- with Charlie Howard. Jule went to Simmons'.

January, Wednesday 13, 1869
Pleasant. Went to school - spelling school tonight. Did not go. Mate is up to Eliza's. She came home at nine o'clock. Stayed all night with me.

January, Thursday 14, 1869
Pleasant - went to school. Albert carried us - went down to the north school house to a meeting. Leslie came home with me. Charles with Mate. Arthur with Florence - had an invite to go to the dance.

Postcard view of a trotting horse and buggy in Jefferson County, New York, circa 1880. Publisher unknown.

January, Friday 15, 1869
Pleasant - went to school. Rode up with Albert. I came at noon. Rode with Albert. I went to the dance with Charlie. I had a good time. Did not get home till five. We won't go home till morning.

January, Saturday 16, 1869
Pleasant. Did not get up till noon. Done the ironing. Mopped the wash room. Swept the chamber. Went down to Florence's. We stayed all night with Mate.

January, Sunday 17, 1869
Pleasant. Ma & Pa went over to Whitneys. Jule came home at night. Did not stay long. See Albert & Charlie go past. Went to bed at eight o'clock. Mate stayed with me. Set upstairs with a bed quilt around us.

January, Monday 18, 1869
Pleasant. Did not go to school. Mrs. Mines and old Mrs. Mines was to our house. I went to [attend to] Mines' birds in the eve. So did Mate.

January, Tuesday 19, 1869
Pleasant - went to school. Went to the Lodge in the eve with Charlie but Mate give Charlie the slip and came home with Albert. I had an invite to go to a French dance but did not go.

January, Wednesday 20, 1869
Colder than the very cold. Harry had an awful time finding my dress. Went to the spelling school. Charlie came home with me. Albert with Mate.

January, Thursday 21, 1869
Cold but pleasant. Went to school. Came home after our arithmetic class. Went to the Donation with Albert White. Melvin & Eve went with us. Had fun. Saw Charlie Mines. He got home the night before. Mate went with Albert Hungerford.

January, Friday 22, 1869
Pleasant - but cold. Went to school. Felt rather sleepy. Got started for home. Met Albert H. & Charlie Howard. Had an invite to go down to [Myron] Ray's to a party. Mate is going with Charlie & I with Albert H.

January, Saturday 23, 1869
Pleasant. Got up at ten o'clock. Done the ironing. Mopped the washroom. Cut off the bottom of my black dress. Went to Ray's party. Saw Ernie, Ebbie, Charlie, Leslie, Harlie, Florence, Ellen. Albert got liquor - was ashamed to think I went.

January, Sunday 24, 1869
Pleasant. Pa & Ma went over to Aunt Dorcas. Wort Whitney was down to our house & spent the eve. Brate [Braton] Snow & Arthur K [Kilby] came there. Charlie H. & Albert H. were there in the afternoon half drunk. Charlie spent the eve over to Mate's.

January, Monday 25, 1869
Pleasant did not go to school. Stayed at home and helped Ma wash. Vic [Victoria] Gleason came and commenced giving me music lessons. Spelling at night. Went. Leslie B. came home with me. Charlie with Mate.

January, Tuesday 26, 1869
Pleasant. Went to school. Mate, Albert White & I went to the Village to go to the Lodge but did not. Instead went to a dance with Charlie H. Pa said his horse wasn't going to take anyone to the Lodge anymore. Mate went with Big Charlie [Howard].

January, Wednesday 27, 1869
Pleasant. Did not go to school. Ma went to the village. Addie & Charlie went over to Orin's. Mate & I went over there. I done my ironing before 9 - went. Charlie & Addie were over to our house a few minutes. The load stopped for Mate & I to go down. Pa wouldn't let me go.

January, Thursday 28, 1869
Pleasant. Went to school. Came home. Started for meeting - heard there was was none but went down there. Arthur came home with Mate. Charlie with Florence, Leslie B [Boyce] with me - we all went to Aunt Julia's - stayed till nine o'clock.

January, Friday 29, 1869
Pleasant. Got the work all done. Went over to Aunt Julia's. Stayed all the forenoon. Ma went down to Seatons'. Mate and I wanted to go to the village, but could not. Saw Albert & Charlie & Mort today.

January, Saturday 30, 1869
Raining a little. Mate & I went down to Mary Ding's a-visiting. Wort Whitney was to our house in the evening. C.D. Howard & Ell Howard also were there. Mate stayed all night. Saw Mort Halladay to day.

January, Sunday 31, 1869
Snowing a little - washed the dishes - went upstairs and went to reading. Mate over here. Arther Kilby spent the eve. Wort Whitney over to Mate's and spent eve.

February, Wednesday 3. 1869.

Snowing and blowing
did not get up till eleven
oclock Went over to aunt
Julias & curled Ma hair
got supper went over to
Mate stayed the eve

Thursday 4.

Snowing and blowing
Mate & I went up to
Miss Bards Charlie came
up there came home
with us Mate stayed
all night with me

Friday 5.

Pleasant did not go to
school Charlie & Carrie
were up and spent the
eve had a good time
Mate stayed all night
with me

February, Saturday 6. 1869.

Pleasant the Hebrews were
over to Aunt Julias a
visiting Julé came home
Florence was up and
spent the eve & went home
with her and stayed
all night

Sunday 7

I went up to the village
Pleasant got home
just as our folks were
going over to Aunt Libs
I was mad because I could
not go Florence up to our
house and stayed all day
Charlie Howard was over to
Aunt Julias in the after noon
Spent the eve to our house

Monday 8.

Pleasant stayed at home
and done the washing
Vic came gave me a lesson
party up to Vandynes
Mate & I went with
Abbie had fun

February, Monday 1, 1869
Pleasant - got the washing done by noon. Practiced two hours [piano] - done the ironing. Went down to Uncle Ed's. Miles Gleason was there. I stayed all night. Ell Vorce stayed with Mate.

February, Tuesday 2, 1869
Pleasant - went to school part of the day. Came home. Practiced an hour. Got ready for the festival. Went with Albert went down to supper with Orlando Bright - had a good time all but Frank Whitney wanted to fight. Got home three o'clock.

February, Wednesday 3, 1869
Snowing and blowing. Did not get up till eleven o'clock. Rosette over to Aunt Julia's. I curled Ma's hair. Got supper. Went over to Mate's - stayed the eve.

February, Thursday 4, 1869
Snowing and blowing. Mate & I went up to Miss Bird's. Harlie came up there. Came home with us. Mate stayed all night with me.

February, Friday 5, 1869
Pleasant. Did not go to school. Harlie & Leslie were up and spent the eve - had a good time. Mate stayed all night with me.

February, Saturday 6, 1869
Pleasant. The Dobsons were over to Aunt Julia's a-hunting. Jule came home. Florence was up and spent the eve. I went home with her and stayed all night.

February, Sunday 7, 1869
I went up to the village with Jule & Albert. Pleasant - got home just as our folks were going over to Aunt Lib's. I was very mad because I could not go. Florence up to our house and stayed all day. Charlie Howard was over to Aunt Julia's in the afternoon. Spent the eve at our house.

February, Monday 8, 1869
Pleasant - stayed at home and done the washing. Vic came - gave me a lesson. Party up to Vandynes. Mate & I went with Albert - had fun.

February, Tuesday 9, 1869
Pleasant - went to school. Stayed all day. Mate went to the Lodge in the eve. Albert Hungerford asked me to go to the Lodge with him but I did not go - wanted to, though.

February, Wednesday 10, 1869
Pleasant. Addie & Charlie. Aunt Dorc & Uncle Charles were to our house a-visiting. Mate & I stayed till noon. Mate stayed with me all night.

February, Thursday 11, 1869
Pleasant - Mate & I went up the Village to stay till Saturday. Went to Delores[?] in the afternoon. Stayed with Jule all night. Mate & I had fun laughing at the men the next morning. Delia & Francis came over to Simmons' while we were there.

February, Friday 12, 1869
Pleasant. Mate & I are to Simmons' a-visiting. Stayed to dinner then went over to school. Went home with Delia Gleason. Went over to the school party - saw Ebbie - stayed with Deal [Delia] all night.

February, Saturday 13, 1869
Raining. Up to Clara Sprague a-visiting. Stayed with Delia Gleason all night and all of the forenoon. went over to Clara's in the afternoon. Aunt Julia was there. Pa came for me to go home before I had supper. Got home and got my things off and Wort came for me to go over to Barney's party.

February, Sunday 14, 1869
Snowing and blowing like fun. Trying to rain & trying to snow. Wish it would do one or the other. Cleared off about dark. Cold enough to freeze the hair on a dog's tail. Brate came down & spent the eve. Had a good time.

February, Monday 15, 1869
Stormed all day. I helped Ma do the washing. Mate is up to the Village yet wish she would come home. Vic came home with Pa. I took a music lesson. Sleepy as Cane [Cain, biblical reference to being tired and unable to sleep].

Postcard view of downtown Henderson, New York, circa 1890. Publisher unknown.

February, Tuesday 16, 1869
Pleasant. Grand old day for the dance but I can't go. Vic is to our house. Charlie H. wanted me to go to the Lodge with him but Pa wouldn't let me go. Went down to Uncle Ed's. Florence came home with me and stayed all night. Mate got home.

February, Wednesday 17, 1869
Pleasant in the morn but stormed about noon. Uncle Richard & Builda are in our house a-visiting. Shellie came and invited Mate and I to go down to Albert W to a party - went - had fun.

February, Thursday 18, 1869
Snowing like fun. Got up and got the breakfast. Done all of the work. Ma has got the headache. Aunt Liza is to our house a-visiting. Mate stayed with me all night.

February, Friday 19, 1869
Snowing like fun. Ma was going up to Mrs. Simmons a-visiting, but had to stay at home and tend to the Jersey cows.

February, Saturday 20, 1869
Pleasant. Ma went to Simmons a-visiting. Mate & I went down to

Uncle Ed's - stayed an hour then went home and got supper then went back. Charlie & Harlie was there. Harlie came up to Aunt Julia's with me.

February, Sunday 21, 1869
Snowing & blowing. Aunt Eliza is over to Julia's. Florence up here in the afternoon. Wort Whitney here in the eve. Brate Snow down to see Florence.

February, Monday 22, 1869
Pleasant - helped Ma wash. Practiced two hours. Vic came in the even - gave me a lesson. Smithville dance I want to go but have had no invite. Mate stayed all night with me.

February, Tuesday 23, 1869
Snowing today. Vic & Pa started for the Village. Had to come back. Rain. Saw Charlie H go by leading his horse, guess he was just getting home from the Smithville dance. Mate stayed with me over night. Practiced two hours.

February, Wednesday 24, 1869
Snowing and blowing like fun. Can't see anyone. Never seen such a day. Ma and I have lots of fun. I have been ironing. Practiced three hours.

February, Thursday 25, 1869
Pleasant - did all of the work. Practiced two hours. Shoveled a path over to Aunt Julia's. Went over there two or three times. Road breakers was out in the afternoon.

February, Friday 26, 1869
Storming - did all of the work. Practiced two hours. Went over to Mate's. Pa got me a letter & Mate one. Mate stayed with me all night.

February, Saturday 27, 1869
Snowing and blowing. Mate & I went down to Uncle Ed's. Aunt Eliza was not at home. Hen Houghton & Jim Seaton came there and spent the eve. I stayed with Mate all night. Big Charlie Howard to our house - [he] came home with Pa.

February, Sunday 28, 1869
Pleasant - got home at eight o'clock. Eat breakfast - washed the dishes. Went over to Aunt Julia's. Came home and set around. Brate Snow came and spent the eve. Wort [came] down to see Florence.

March, Monday 1, 1869
Pleasant. Mate & I did the washing. Went over to Aunt Susan's in the afternoon. Mary Ding & Arthur were there a-visiting. Victoria, Jule & Pa came. Jim came at dark. I took a lesson.

March, Tuesday 2, 1869
Pleasant. Practiced an hour in the afternoon. Went down to school. Came back. Stopped to Aunt Susan's to tea. Frank Dobson & Mother & Aunt were there. Mate, Aunt Jule, there too. Harlie & Leslie spent the eve here.

March, Wednesday 3, 1869
Pleasant. Did all the work. Practiced two hours in the afternoon. Mate & I went down to Rosette's. Florence was there. Albert H came over after Mate to go down to Vorces to a rehearsal so we went. Flora & I. Jim & Charlie brought us home.

March, Thursday 4, 1869
Pleasant. Stayed at home all day. Practiced two hours. Mate went to school. Came home and stayed all night with me.

March, Friday 5, 1869
Pleasant in the morning. Mate & I went over to Addie's with Pa. I stayed all day. In the evening I went to Warner's to a dance. Stayed till 4 o'clock. Addie & Charlie did not stay long. Mate went with Albert Hungerford. I went with Wort Whitney.

March, Saturday 6, 1869
Snowing & blowing. Did not get home till eight o'clock. Practiced two hours. About 3 o'clock Wesley Vandyne [lived next door] came after me to go up there. Lucy [Vandyne] was sick. Went. Olive Gill called there.

From *History of Jefferson County, New York,* 1878 page 378B.

RES. OF G. W. COLLINS, HENDERSON, JEFFERSON CO., N.Y.

From *History of Jefferson County, New York*, 1878 page 380A.

March, Sunday 7, 1869
Pleasant. Got up and did all the work. Lucy is a little better. Got the bread ready to bake then Wes came and brought me home after supper. I went down to Florence's. Flo came a piece with me.

March, Monday 8, 1869
Pleasant. Ma & I did the washing. Got all through by noon. Victoria & Pa came just [at] dark. Aunt Eliza is here. Florence & Charlie Howard came here. Charlie did not stay only a few minutes.

March, Tuesday 9, 1869
Pleasant- stayed at home all day. Practices two hours. Saw Wort & Wesley go by. Grand night for the Lodge but I can't go. Aunt Julia is going. Turned Ernie C, Charley H, Wort W, Bill Taylor out of the Lodge. Good thing I guess.

March, Wednesday 10, 1869
Snowing & blowing - just putting in its best licks. Mate did not go to school. Practiced two hours. Read two or three stories. Played backgammon with Everett. Have had a good time all around.

March, Thursday 11, 1869
Trying to snow but has not made out to yet. Mate has gone to school. Practiced two hours . Got the toothache and the devil's to pay in general. David spent the evening. Stayed with Ell all night.

March, Friday 12, 1869
Pleasant. Last day of school. Exhibition in the eve. I was down to Uncle Ed's all day. Flora & I went to the exhibition. So many there. The performance could not go on. Came pretty near [to] having a fight.

March, Saturday 13, 1869
Snowing a little. Ell & I went over to Snows. Only fourteen of us there. Had a gay time. Stayed till eleven o'clock. Ell Whitney & Lucy, Mate, Ell Vorce, Albert Hungerford & Byron was there.

March, Sunday 14, 1869
Pleasant. Stayed at home. Ma & Pa went down to Uncle Ed's. Flo came up here. Jennie Lovell took us riding. Went down to Vorces. Em & Jim were there. Brate spent the eve here. Had a good visit.

March, Monday 15, 1869
Pleasant. Jule & I washed. Victoria came just at dark.

March, Tuesday 16, 1869
Jule & I all alone. Ma visited Mrs. Ebbie Kilby. Victoria came about four o'clock. Elvira Boyce is here.

March, Wednesday 17, 1869
Pleasant - went down to Uncle Ed's and stayed all night. Mrs. Johnson was buried today. Aunt Eliza went to the funeral so Flo & me had a good time.

March, Thursday 18, 1869
Pleasant - did all of the work. Went to the village. Flora & I went to Spragues then went to the last day of school had fun. Charlie H. was three sheets in the wind. Felt pretty well, I guess.

March, Friday 19, 1869
Pleasant. Got up at eight o'clock. Eat breakfast. Went down to Mr. Eggleston's with Florence. Marie S is to Spragues'. Uncle Ed came after us at four o'clock. Jennie [younger sister] stayed all night to Seatons tonight.

March, Saturday 20, 1869
Pleasant. Stayed at home all day. Mate came home a few minutes with Charlie Howard. Jule came home with Pa. Jennie came too.

March, Sunday 21, 1869
Pleasant. Flora & Charlie came up here. Ma & Pa went to to the Harbor about dark. Jule & I went a piece with C.H. Brate Snow & Frank Whitney came along. Went down to Flora's and spent the eve.

114   JEFFERSON COUNTY DIRECTORY.

HENDERSON VILLAGE.
Population—500

Boots and Shoes.
E O Kilby
W W Gleason

Blacksmiths.
Allen Kilby
Samuel Peters
Levi Halladay

Bowling Saloon.
Benj Fuller

Butcher.
B C Seaton

Carpenters.
A F Lawrence
J W Barnes
A G Lawrence

Carriage Makers.
E Brown
H T Halladay

Cheese Box Maker
Valentine Parker

Cheese Factory.
Elmon Tyler

Clergyman.
Rev G A Dougherty, Bpt

Collector Customs.
M Wilkinson

Constables.
B C Seaton
A Brooke
Albert Haskins
W Young

Cooper.
D H Cole

Dress Makers.
Mrs M E Eggleston
Mrs Celia Boomer

Furniture Dealers.
Bates & Sawyer
  H P Bates
  C F Sawyer

General Merchants
L B Simmons
J M White & Co
  J M White
  C G Mixer
  A J Armstrong

Groceries.
Sprague Bros
  F A Sprague
  C H Sprague

Harness Maker.
E O Kilby

Hotels.
Exchange, W A Halladay, Proprietor.
Burnham's Hotel, Wm Burnham, Proprietor

Lawyers.
A A Davis
H P Bates

Machinist.
J H VanWinckel

C. N. RUSSELL & CO'S
Rectifying House,

PLAIN AND FANCY WHISKIES,

Imported Liquors and Wines,

Alcohol, Pure Domestic Wines, &c.

21 PUBLIC SQUARE, WATERTOWN, N. Y.

Baker & Chittenden,
No. 5, Arcade, WATERTOWN, N. Y.,
Wholesale and Retail Dealers in

TOBACCO, SNUFF, CIGARS,
Hunting & Fishing Tackle.
GENERAL FIRE, LIFE, MARINE AND ACCIDENT
Insurance Agents.
GENERAL TICKET AG'TS
for all Railroad and Steamboat Lines to the West, Canada, Europe and California. Business hours from 6 A. M. to 10 P. M. Drafts sold on all Foreign Countries.

CHAS. E. GOULD,
Manufacturer and Dealer in
Tin, Copper and Sheet Iron Ware,
PARLOR, COOK AND BOX STOVES,
Eaves Troughs Milk Cans, Sap Pans,
&c., &c., &c.,
CAREFULLY MADE TO ORDER,
FROM FIRST QUALITY STOCK.
PHILADELPHIA, - - - New York.

This page and opposite, from *Gazetteer and directory of Jefferson County, New York*, for 1866-7. Watertown, N.Y.: I Ingalls & Co., Printer and Bookbinders, 1866, Child, Hamilton.

RALPH HOOKER,

IN GALLAGHER'S BLOCK,

CARTHAGE, NEW YORK,

GENERAL DEALER IN FOREIGN & DOMESTIC

DRY GOODS

GROCERIES,

Hardware, Cloths,

BOOTS & SHOES,

YANKEE NOTIONS!

The best assortment of Family Groceries always on hand.

Dress Goods, Mohairs, Cashmeres, Delaines, French and English Merinoes, Silks, Prints, Hoop Skirts,

Flannels, Broadcloths, Ladies' Cloths, Table Linen, Bleach'd Goods, Ladies Cloaks, Broche Shawls, Balmorals,

Constantly on hand and for sale at the lowest cash price, a large stock of

Sugars,
Teas,
Coffees,
Molasses,
Spices,
Syrups,
Flour,
Pork,
Fish,

Candles,
Soap,
Salt,
Lard,
Meal,
Raisins,
Rice,
&c., &c.

ALSO A LARGE STOCK OF

CROCKERY, GLASS WARE,

KEROSENE OIL, &C., &C.

Haying Utensils Always on Hand.

All Kinds of Barter Taken in Exchange.

CASH PAID FOR BUTTER.

ORDERS SOLICITED. — — — SATISFACTION WARRANTED.

P. HOOKER.

Post Master.
L B Simmons
Saw-Mills.
V Parker
S H Weeks
Supervisor.
Wm Dobson
Surveyor.
H W Davis
Teleg'h Operator.
W W Gleason

ROBERTS CORNERS.
(See Index)

SMITHVILLE.
(See under head of Adams.)

HOUNSFIELD.
EAST HOUNSFIELD.
Blacksmith.
Samuel Roberts
Carpenter.
Nelson Jones
Constable.
Schuyler Lewis
Dress Maker.
Mrs Chas Brimmer
Hotel.
Wm Warren
Post Master.
Marvin Scoville
Shoemaker.
Thos Warren

SACKETS HARBOR.
Population—about 1,200.
Agricultur'l Implements.
David McKee
Auctioneer.
John Parker
Bakery.
J Phelps & Co
Jason Phelps }
Irvin J Phelps }
Billiard Rooms.
Jacob Bass
Oscar P Button
Blacksmiths.
Richard Boyd
John Perrigo
Joel Smith
Boat Builder.
Alanson Fields
Books and Stat'y.
Daniel S Kimball
Boots and Shoes.
Robert Baker
Geo Butterfield
C Lane & Son
Chas Lars }
Henry J Lane }
David Palmer
Wm Wiley

March 22, 1869
Pleasant - helped ma wash. Stayed at home all day. Mont Sprague went up to the village with Pa. Stayed all night. Pretty late for beans.

March 23, 1869
Pleasant. Got the headache. Can't hardly breath. Practiced two hours. Did the ironing. Ma went up to Mrs. Cranage's. Stayed all night.

March 24, 1869
Mary Dings got a letter. Pleasant. Got up and did breakfast. Ma up to Mrs. Cranage's yet. Made up Aunt Julia's bed and swept for her. She is down to Dings. Went down to Flora's. Frank H and Ell Vorce spent the eve here.

March 25, 1869
Pleasant. Ma went over to Sim [Simeon] Danley's a-visiting. I went down to Florence's in the eve. Got home and Mate was here - just got home from Champion [a nearby town].

March, Friday 26, 1869
Raining. Wanted to go over to Ed Whitney's but Uncle Wash [Washington] wouldn't let Mate go so we stayed at home. Mate stayed with me all night.

March, Saturday 27, 1869
Pleasant. Went over to Mate's. Stayed all of the afternoon. She can't stay with me anymore nights - Uncle Wash says he is an old drunk and everybody knows it. Florence stayed with me all night.

March, Sunday 28, 1869
Pleasant but pretty slushy underfoot - as Harlie says. Florence up here all day & Aunt Eliza & Ed. Mate, Florence & I went up to Bird's [Birdsall Boyce?]. Florence went home about dark. Bad night for beans Florence & I think.

March, Monday 29, 1869
Pleasant some of the time. Pa went to Watertown. Ma & I washed. Albert [younger brother] went to the Village.

March, Tuesday 30, 1869
Stormy. Mate & I went up to Mrs. Bird's in the afternoon. Had a good visit. Mate stayed at home - so did I all night.

March, Wednesday 31, 1869
Pleasant. Mate & I went down to Uncle Ed's. Stayed all night. David & Arthur Kilby spent the eve there - did not have a very good time. Arthur was all out of sorts, sleepy, and everything - they just set and giggled all the time.

April, Thursday 1, 1869
Pleasant. Got up at six o'clock. Flora & I got breakfast - tried to fool Mate & Aunt Liza - got fooled ourselves. Addie Eggleston [cousin] here a-visiting. I stayed all night with Flora.

April, Friday 2, 1869
Pleasant. Got home at six o'clock. Stayed at home all of the forenoon. Went over to Aunt Julia's in the afternoon. Charlie & Harlie & David Montague spent the eve here. Mate stayed all night with me.

April, Saturday 3, 1869
Pleasant. Got home at six o'clock. Stayed at home all of the forenoon. Went over to Aunt Julia's in the afternoon. Big Charlie H, Harlie, & Leslie spent the eve here. Mate stayed all night with me. Pa got home from Watertown - eleven o'clock.

April, Sunday 4, 1869
Not so very pleasant. Mate is over here. We went up to Elvira's - stayed about an hour - got a letter from Jule she wrote Florence - had been telling some thing. Went to bed at eight o'clock. Wort W called but did not stay.

April, Monday 5, 1869
Pleasant - but cold. Have got to wash. Wish I hadn't got to though. Victoria came home with Pa. Gave me a lesson.

No entries for April 6 - 9, 1869

April, Saturday 10, 1869
Pleasant. Practiced an a hour. Went down and stayed with Florence all night.

April, Sunday 11, 1869
Pleasant. Mate & I went up to Elvira's a little while. Mate went down to Aunt Eliza's and stayed all night. David Montague spent the eve here. Where will I be in ten years from today?

April, Monday 12, 1869
Albert [younger brother] went off [sailing] this morning. Not so very pleasant. I did most of the washing. Practiced an hour. Went to bed at half past eight. Victoria did not come. Pa did not get home till ten o'clock. David Montague went to Colorado.

April, Tuesday 13, 1869
Pleasant - stayed at home till night. Then went down and stayed all night with Florence.

April, Wednesday 14, 1869
Pleasant - stayed at home all day. At night went down to Florence's and stayed all night.

April, Thursday 15, 1869
Pleasant. Mate & I went up to the Village. Today's is Teacher's examination. We stayed to Mrs. Eggleston's all night with Jule. Saw the boys ride the velocipede. Mr. Borden & Connelly. Mont Sprague's father harvested today.

April, Friday 16, 1869
Mate & I got home at nine o'clock. Ma was just going over to the Harbor. Mate is over here - it is the warmest day I ever see. Just like summer. Stayed with Florence all night.

April, Saturday 17, 1869
Raining. Mate & I came home at nine o'clock. Jen [younger sister] & I went to the Corners for our molasses. Pa is fifty years old today. Florence & I run away down to Rosette's.

April, Sunday 18, 1869
Raining in the morning. I stayed at home until night. Went down and stayed all night with Florence. Got a letter from Albert tonight. Wort Whitney called to see Flora & me.

April, Monday 19, 1869
Pleasant. Ma & I washed. Got through by noon. Victoria came at night. Gave me a lesson.

April, Tuesday 20, 1869
Pleasant. Got up at five o'clock. Practiced two hours and a half. Ma is over to Aunt Susan's a-visiting with Aunt Eliza. Florence is down to Rosette's. Raining like fun.

April, Wednesday 21, 1869
Not very pleasant. I stayed at home until noon then went over to Aunt Julia's and stayed all the afternoon. Went down to Florence's - stayed all night. Jane Hicks was there to have her ears pierced. Saw Harlie Howard.

April, Thursday 22, 1869
Pleasant. Got home at nine o'clock. Practiced a little while. Got dinner. Florence is going tomorrow. Oh, dear what shall I do after she is gone. I went down to Mary Dings then Florence stayed all night with me.

April, Friday 23, 1869
Pleasant. Got up at nine o'clock. Got ready for Adams [town]. Flora and I rode with Orange [Vandyne]. Mate and Eliza went with Old Dol [horse] and the buggy. Mate and I had our pictures taken. Saw Hen Houghton. Mary Dings is very rich.

April, Saturday 24, 1869
Pleasant. Stayed at home. Mate went up to Mrs. Bird's. I stayed with her all night. Practiced nearly two hours.

April, Sunday 25, 1869
Pleasant but rather cold. Mate is over here. Uncle Washington came home today. Aunt Julia has gone down to Mary's. Brate Snow spent the eve here.

April, Monday 26, 1869
Not very pleasant. Ma & I washed. Victoria did not come. I stayed at home all night. Got a letter from Florence.

April, Tuesday 27, 1869
Pleasant. Ma & I cleaned the chamber did not get through until night. Pa give me a new [music] piece "Sack Waltz."

April, Wednesday 28, 1869
Pleasant. Pa & Vic went away at seven o'clock. Ma & I cleaned the pantry. Did not get through till night. Then Mate & I went to the Corners. I saw a magic lantern [show]. Albert Hungerford. Came home with Mate.

April, Thursday 29, 1869
Pleasant. Uncle William is painting the dining room. I am not doing much of anything practical. A little while went over to Aunt Julia's. Mate is down to her Aunt Abigail's.

April, Friday 30, 1869
Pleasant. Uncle Will is painting. Practiced a little while. Jule came home with Pa. Went over to Aunt Julia's. Came home. Harlie came up after us to go sailing. Had fun.

May, Saturday 1, 1869
Pleasant. Jule went back to the Village. Practiced a little while. Mate over here.

May, Sunday 2, 1869
Raining. Mate is over here. I finished Jen's dress. It is no sin to sew on Sunday if one is obliged. We went over to Aunt Julia's. Harlie came here and spent the eve.

May, Monday 3, 1869.
Ma & I washed. Washed all of the windows in the parlor & kitchen. Vic came before I got through mopping. Gave me a lesson.

"The Sack Waltz" was written by John A. Metcalf in 1862.

Tuesday 4, May 1869

Pleasant. practiced two hours went over to Aunts Julias came home did not do much of any thing oh yes washed the dishes

Wednesday 5

Pleasant. Mrs Howard Hattie & I went across the bay in a boat then Mrs H & I went to the village got there and bound Edeth we went down to the grocery saw Ernie C Frank B. then rode home with Olive Gill got a letter from H.

Thursday 6

Pleasant. Addie got up and got breakfast did the work then Addie and I went down to the Grocery saw Dannie Gill came home at noon with Mrs Howard & Hattie on a boat. Oranage Hatties Chum was with us

Friday 7, May 1869

Pleasant. did not do much of any thing Hattie & I went down to Marions school to the mouth of the creek stoped to Uncle Richards when we came back stayed the evening had tea stayed with Kate all night

Saturday 8

Pleasant. Uncle Richard and Matilda were here did not stay long after they went away I went down to Mrs Howards but could not find Hattie & Kate came home got supper for old Mrs Howard

Sunday 9

Pleasant. Hattie came up before I got my dishes washed for us to go sailing went down to that Bayees & Ernie & Bell went and took a sail there Hattie & I helped him strip his boat went a pice with him to the corners then Albert H took us all to the village

May, Tuesday 4, 1869
Pleasant. Practiced two hours. Went over to Aunt Julia's. Came home. Did not do much of anything. Oh yes, we cleaned the parlor.

May, Wednesday 5, 1869
Pleasant. Mrs. Howard Martin and I went across the bay in a boat. Then Mrs. H. & I went to the Village. Got there and found Addie. We went down to the grocery. Saw Ernie C, Frank K, then rode home with Olive Gill [sister-in-law or mother-in-law?]. Got a letter from Florence.

May, Thursday 6, 1869
Pleasant. Addie got up and got breakfast. Did the work then Addie and I went down to the grocery. Saw Dannie Gill. Came home at noon with Mrs. Howard & Harlie on a boat. Cranage, Harlie's chum, was with us.

May, Friday 7, 1869
Pleasant. Did not do much of anything. Harlie & I went down to Marian's school to the mouth of the creek. Stopped to ---ndy when we came back. Stayed the evening. Had fun. I stayed with Mate all night.

May, Saturday 8, 1869
Pleasant. Uncle Richard and Builda were here. Did not stay long. After they away I went down to Mrs. Howard's but could not find Mate & Harlie. Came home - got supper for old Mrs. Nealy.

May, Sunday 9, 1869
Pleasant. Harlie came up before I got my dishes washed - for us to go sailing - went down to Wat Boyce's & Anice & Bell went and took a sail then Mate & I helped him strip his boat. Went a piece with him to the Corners then Albert H took us all to the Village.

May, Monday 10, 1869
Pleasant. Mate & I washed. Did not get through until afternoon. I went over to Aunt Julia's and read all rest of the afternoon. Practiced a few minutes in the eve.

May, Tuesday 11, 1869
Pleasant - Ma & I took up the carpet. Dusted it and put it down again. Victoria came with Pa. I had gone to bed - so got rid of taking a lesson.

May, Wednesday 12, 1869
Pleasant. Got my ironing done by noon. I've never seen such a warm day. Aunt Julia is coloring. Orange [Vandyne], Aunt Susan called here a few minutes. I practiced a little while. Went to bed at eight o'clock. Took my last minute lesson.

May, Thursday 13, 1869
Pleasant - practiced a little while. Cut the skirt of my buff calico dress. I tore a ball of carpet rags. Got supper.

May, Friday 14, 1869
Raining this morn. Aunt Julia & I went over to Ellisburg. Saw Em Snow. Mate came home with us. Saw Elvira. Mr. Fry is here tuning our piano.

May, Saturday 15, 1869
Pleasant. Mate is over here. Aunt Mary Vorce is here a-visiting. Mate is making pies after and I am making my buff calico dress. Got a letter from Florence, Charles Ellis & Albert White.

May, Sunday 16, 1869
Raining. Mate over here. We had a good old chat then went to bed & Wort Whitney came. Mate & Jule. Guess Mate & I did not see Wort when he came. Oh, no.

May, Monday 17, 1869
Cold & raining. I went down to the creek and drove Old Fan for Mate. Got home at ten o'clock. Swept the dining room, washed the dinner and supper dishes. Went to bed at dark.

May, Tuesday 18, 1869
Pleasant. Victoria came with Addie Walker. Jule had got ready for the Village but had to stay at home.

May, Wednesday 19, 1869
Pleasant. Vic stayed all day with us and learned Jule and me to -----. We commenced our night dresses.

May, Thursday 20, 1869
Pleasant. Jule & I are at work at our night dresses. Got one side of mine done.

May, Friday 21, 1869
Pleasant. Stayed at home. Lucy Vandyne was here a-visiting. Aunt Jule went after Mate. After I got to bed Mate came over to the gate and we talked quite a long while.

May, Saturday 22, 1869
Pleasant. Jule & I went to the Village with Pa. From there down to the Harbor with Brown. Mrs. Whitney was over to Addie's. We all went to the Village a-foot. Rode home with Pa.

May, Sunday 23, 1869
Pleasant. Mate, Jule & I went up to Elvira's and stayed all day. Came home about six o'clock. Mate came down to see Jule. Ernie drink Chepenna [champagne?] Saw Frank Whitney and Katie Barrett.

May, Monday 24, 1869
Pleasant. Jule did most of the washing. I carried Mate to the creek then came - got dinner. Vic come with Pa. Jule & I had gone to bed when they got here.

May, Tuesday 25, 1869
Pleasant. Ma & Aunt Julia went over to Aunt Elizabeth's. Vic stayed with Jule and me. Aunt Susan, Jule & I went to the Village. Saw Mont, Brate, Dan Gill and lots of others.

May, Wednesday 26, 1869
Pleasant in the forenoon. I carried Vic up to the Walkers. Then went from there down to the creek to Mate's school. Ellen V. Went with me. Raining this afternoon.

May, Thursday 27, 1869
Pleasant. Ma & Jule have gone to Smithville and I have got to stay all alone. Wish Mate was at home. I have written to C.R. Ellis this afternoon. Milked Aunt Julia's cow and our own. Ma has not got home yet.

May, Friday 28, 1869
Pleasant in the morning but commenced raining in the afternoon. Took Fanny and went down to the Creak after Mate. Rained on the way there and back.

May, Saturday 29, 1869
Raining - stayed with Mate last night. Got home. Our folks were eating. Rosette is over to Aunt Julia's. Doctor Chapman called here. I was over there a few minutes.

May, Sunday 30, 1869
Pleasant. Stayed with Mate last night. Got up this morn at seven o'clock. Basted Mate's ruffle on her dress. Came home. Went out riding with Brate Snow. Went to Woodville. Jule came home. Mont brought her.

May, Monday 31, 1869
Pleasant. Jule & I washed. Did not get through till four o'clock.

June, Tuesday 1, 1869
Pleasant. Albert came home with Victoria & Pa. Jule & I went to the Village. Saw Anna Nugent. Shows to the Village tonight - but did not go.

June, Wednesday 2, 1869
Pleasant. Victoria stayed here all day. At night, Jule & I went and took her home. Saw Everett Hollis. Went to bed as soon as we got home.

June, Thursday 3, 1869
Pleasant - Jule & I hung the clothes out. Went to Adams [town] to carry Albert. Stayed and went to the circus with Mont. Eva & Hollie were there, Ada, Elva, George, Barney, Ernie, Myron & Jennie.

MAY, FRIDAY 28. 1869.

Pleasant in the morn
but commenced rain
in the after noon I
took Fanny and went
down to the Creek
after Mate rained all
the way there and back

SATURDAY 29.

Raining stayed with
Mate last night got
home ou Folks were
eating Rosett is over
to Aunt Jules Doctor
Chaf man called
there I was over there
a few minutes

SUNDAY 30.

Pleasant stayed with
Mate last night got up
this morn at eleven o
clock Bartee Mate Riggl
on his dray Emma Fany
went out riding with
Bruce Enny went to
azord ville Jule came
home Mate brought her

MAY, MONDAY 31. 1869.

Pleasant Jule & I
washed did
not get through till
four oclock

JUNE, TUESDAY 1.

Pleasant Albert came
home with Victoria
& Pa Jule & I went
to the Village saw
Anna Van gort
spoke to the Village
to night but did
not go

WEDNESDAY 2.

Pleasant Victoria stayed
here all day at night
Jule & I went and took
her home saw Evert
Hollie went to bed
as soon as we got
home

RES. OF MRS. T. O. WHITNEY, HENDERSON, JEFFERSON CO., N.Y.

From *History of Jefferson County, New York*, 1878 page 388A.

From *History of Jefferson County, New York*, 1878 page 382A.

June, Friday 4, 1869
Pleasant in the morning. Ma, Jule & I went up to Lucy Vandyne's a-visiting. I went down and got Mate. Joe Finney was to school. Raining just as we came back.

June, Saturday 5, 1869
Raining and foggy. Mate came over to have Ma stitch her skirt. Aunt Julia is over here. Raining yet. Mate over here this eve. Pa came home rather out-of-sorts - little mad. I guess because it rains.

June, Sunday 6, 1869
Pleasant. Mate, Jule & I went out to the clearing. Saw some boys - we did not know who they were though they asked us to take a sail and said "be damned" if we did not know them. Girls went down to see Jule.

June, Monday 7, 1869
Pleasant. Jule & I washed. Ma & Uncle William moved the stove. Elvira Boyce is here a-visiting. Carrie Worthingham, the teacher, is boarding here this week. Jule is practicing. Jule & I did not have any company.

June, Tuesday 8, 1869
Pleasant. Vic is here. Stayed all day.

June, Wednesday 9, 1869
Pleasant. Vic went up to Walkers. Stayed at home all day. Carrie is here.

June, Thursday 10, 1869
Raining. Jule & I ironed all day. Mrs. Ray was here a few minutes & Miss Baz--- . Carrie here at night.

June, Friday 11, 1869
Pleasant. Jule & Aunt Julia went over to Ellisburgh. Mate came home with them. Got a letter form Charles Ellis.

June, Saturday 12, 1869
Pleasant. Finished my night dress. Mopped the washroom. Practiced a little while. Mate over here.

June, Sunday 13, 1869
Not very pleasant. Jule & I rode a-horse back.

June, Monday 14, 1869
Pleasant but cold as the devil. Carrie, Jule & I went fishing and caught an eel. Had fun.

June, Tuesday 15, 1869
Raining like fun. Jule & I was going up to the village but could not. Vic is here.

June, Wednesday 16, 1869
Cold but never the less Carrie, Jule & I went fishing. Carrie caught an eel. I came home before the rest because I was cold.

June, Thursday 17, 1869
Pleasant. Jule & I hung the clothes out. Saw the *Comet* and Laura Gleason go by & Doctor Barney.

No entries for June 18 - 20, 1869

June, Monday 21, 1869
Pleasant. Jule & washed. Got through at noon. Practiced a little. Vic came at night with Pa. We were down fishing. I caught an eel.

June, Tuesday 22, 1869
Not very pleasant in the morning. Stayed at home all day. Aunt Julia & Jule & I were down fishing. I went to the Corners a-horse back. Willie Crittenden asked me to go to the dance.

June, Wednesday 23, 1869
Pleasant. We went to Walkers this morn. Jule & I went up to the Village after Pa. I rode with Earl Green. Met Uncle Richard & Builda. Saw Delia Gleason.

June, Thursday 24, 1869
Pleasant. Stayed at home all day and ironed. Practiced a little while.

June, Friday 25, 1869
Pleasant. Got up at breakfast. Put the carpet down in the bedroom upstairs. Mate Lawrence & Brate Snow called here. Brate & I took a ride.

June, Saturday 26, 1869
Pleasant. Jule, Mate & I went up to the Village. Stayed till eleven o'clock. Mate rode down to the Dickey Hill with us. Came alone the rest of the way.

June, Sunday 27, 1869
Raining like fun. Jule & I did not get up till breakfast was ready. Eat our breakfast and went back to bed again. Lucy & Wes came down and we had to get up - was mad as fury. Rode down to Peter's with Mate & Jule. Wort called here. Earl Green invited me to the dance with him.

June, Monday 28, 1869
Pleasant. Jule & I washed. Got through by noon. We came with Pa in the eve.

June, Tuesday 29, 1869
Pleasant. Jule, Vic & I was down to Mrs. Gleason's. In the eve Delia, Jule & I went to the Village. Earl brought me home. Mate rode home with Jule & Deal.

June, Wednesday 30, 1869
Not very pleassant. Delia went home this morning. Vic was up to Mr. Walker's. Went with Pa in the morning.

July, Thursday 1, 1869
Pleasant. Did not get up till breakfast was ready. Jule was sewing on my dress. Charlie Mines came and wanted her to go up to Mrs. Burnham's. She went - come down with Earl and went to the dance with us. Did not get home until daylight.

July, Friday 2, 1869
Pleasant. Did not get [up] until noon. Eat my dinner. Ironed and mopped the washroom. Leslie Vandyne was down here. Mate came home. I stayed all night with her.

July, Saturday 3, 1869
Not very pleasant. Mate & I went up to the Village with Pa. Went down to the Harbor with Mr. Brown. Went down to Aunt Dork's. Jule & Mate, May & Earl came over there. I went over to the Hotel [Frontier Hotel] with them and on the steamer Earl brought me home.

July, Sunday 4, 1869
Pleasant. Mate stayed here all night last night and all day today. I expected Brate Snow down here this eve. He did not come. Jule & I carried Mate to the Village after ten o'clock.

July, Monday 5, 1869
Pleasant. Jule & I washed. Did not get through till after noon. Vic did not come tonight. Jule & I went to bed at dark.

July, Tuesday 6, 1869
Pleasant. Did not get up till breakfast was ready. Stayed at home all day. Wanted to go to the Village but Cranage was using Old Charly.

July, Wednesday 7, 1869
Pleasant - stayed at home all day. Elvira Boyce was down here. Mort & Jennie Ivory called and stayed the eve. Jule & I looked like thunder.

July, Thursday 8, 1869
Pleasant - stayed at home all day. Earl Green & Charlie Mines was down here a few minutes. I had a ride in Earl's new buggy. Went to bed at dark.

July, Friday 9, 1869
Pleasant - stayed at home all day in the afternoon. Henry Houghton & John Ivory came here and called a few minutes.

July, Saturday 10, 1869
Pleasant. Jule & I washed a few things. Had fun. Got to work at noon when Dolla Halliday and Charles Partridge came - they did not get out. Myron & Earl spent the eve here.

Postcard view of the Henderson Harbor hotel, circa 1890. Publisher unknown.

July, Sunday 11, 1869
Pleasant but the wind blows a perfect gale. Jule & I carried Mate to Nick Vorce's. Met Albert H just going down there. Darn Brate Snow - he did not come tonight. Mate is here as usual.

July, Monday 12, 1869
Pleasant. Got up and did the work - all of the washing, mopped the wood house and washroom, ironed all of the clothes, swept the chamber, and played ball with Everett. Jule has gone to the Village with Lucy Vandyne.

July, Tuesday 13, 1869
Pleasant. Ma, Jule & Aunt Julia went to the Village to Mrs. Burnham's funeral. Ma got home at five o'clock. Jule has not come yet. I went up to Bird's a little while. Mont brought Jule home.

July, Wednesday 14, 1869
Pleasant. Stayed at home until night then Aunt Julia & I went to Uncle Bill Wilkinson's after some gooseberries. Shellie [Charles Rounds] helped me look mine over.

July, Thursday 15, 1869
Pleasant. Jule & I went up stairs and went to bed. Shellie called here a few minutes. Then went to the Corners. Then came back - Shellie & I went down to the creek. Mate & Albert was out riding. We came home & Shellie spent the eve here.

July, Friday 16, 1869
Pleasant. Aunt Jule went after Mate. Saw Shellie go past. Mate came here.

July, Saturday 17, 1869
Pleasant. Jule went up to Lucy's. Went up to the Village. Mate & I run around. Went down to Harlie's. Coming home got a ride with Albert H. We told him to come down the next day and go sailing.

July, Sunday 18, 1869
Pleasant. Harlie, Albert Hungerford, Jule, Mate & I went out sailing. Went down to the end of the Point. Went ashore. Did not get home very early. Mate & Earl Green spent the eve. Charlie Partridge & Ell Whitney called.

July, Monday 19, 1869
Pleasant. Jule & I washed. Did not get through till noon.

July, Tuesday 20, 1869
Pleasant. Ironed. Vic was here. She went down to Gleasons. Jule went up to the Village with Br-- & I went with Aunt Susan. Charlie Partridge was going to bring me home but it rained.

July, Wednesday 21, 1869
Colder than fury. Stayed at home all day. Jule came home with Pa. Charlie Partridge & Mont spent the eve here - had a very good time. Aunt Julia & I picked cherries down to Uncle Ed's.

July, Thursday 22, 1869
Pleasant. I took Old Charlie and went after Vic. She stopped here and gave me a lesson. Then Jule & I took her up to Walkers. We stopped and seen Lucy swarm bees.

July, Friday 23, 1869
Pleasant. Aunt Julia, Aunt Susan, Jule, & I went down to Uncle Ed's to get some cherries. They had a row with Millie and a devil of a time. She swore at us and everything else.

July, Saturday 24, 1869
Pleasant. Mate & I stayed over to Aunt Julia's all the afternoon. At night we went up the road - run around a while - came home and found Harlie stringing with Everett.

July, Sunday 25, 1869
Pleasant. Mate, Leslie, Harlie, Jule & I went to the high rocks a-fishing. Did not get home until night. Brate called here but I was not at home. Mate & Charlie Partridge spent the eve.

July, Monday 26, 1869
Pleasant. Jule & I washed. Did not get through until afternoon. Then we went to bed and slept until night.

July, Tuesday 27, 1869
Pleasant. Vic is here. We practiced all day. Mate wanted to go to the Village but could not, so I stayed at home.

July, Wednesday 28, 1869
Pleasant. Jule & Aunt Julia went down to the Nick Vorce's to pick cherries. I carried Vic up to Mr. Walker's this morn. Clara Sprague rode home with me.

July, Thursday 29, 1869
Pleasant. Aunt Julia & I went down to Nick Vorce's to pick cherries. Got home at five o'clock. Had just got the cherries pitted when Charlie Partridge called and spent the eve. Ernie went down to see Em.

July, Friday 30, 1869
Pleasant. Aunt Julia went to the creek after Mate. Ma went with her and they went to Mrs. Bullfinch's a-visiting. I did Aunt Julia's chores for her. I was glad when I got home.

July, Saturday 31, 1869
Pleasant. After we got the work did, Mate & I went up to the Corners to the last day of school. Went over to Lucy's to tea. Did not get home till nine o'clock. Mate & I had our hair all down on our backs. Charles Partridge spent the eve. We went over to Ell Whitney's.

August, Sunday 1, 1869
Pleasant. Mate & I took some books and went out to the clearing and read - from there went down to Uncle Ed's after some cherries. Harlie asked us to go and have a sail but the wind blew too hard. Saw Delia, Leslie & Belle go by.

August, Monday 2, 1869
Pleasant. I did most of the washing. Got through by noon. Went to bed. Slept two hours then got up and mopped the washroom. Pa for-

got to bring Vic. Aunt Julia & I went down to Rosette's. Saw Leslie & Harlie.

August, Tuesday 3, 1869
Pleasant. Vic came about nine o'clock. Her father brought her. Ma, Vic & I went up to Elvira's. She had been to Ellisburgh with Rosette.

August, Wednesday 4, 1869
Pleasant. This morning Aunt Susan & Aunt Julia is over here. I was intending to go to Belleville but is raining so I had to stay at home. Saw Harlie & Leslie go by. Jen & I was out picking the raspberries. Saw Delia go by.

August, Thursday 5, 1869
Pleasant but cold. Aunt Julia has company. I stayed at home until six o'clock then went down to the lighthouse with Charlie Partridge. Got home at nine o'clock. Charlie spent the eve.

August, Friday 6, 1869
Pleasant. Aunt Julia & I went raspberrying this morning. Had just got home when Alice P-- and her mother came. I went down to Peter Demell's with them in the afternoon. Mrs. Reed and Mrs. Snow were at our house a-visiting [when] we all came home.

August, Saturday 7, 1869
Pleasant. Get up to breakfast. Head hurt. Got the work done when Addie & Aunt Dorcus came. Stayed here in the forenoon. Went over to Aunt Julia's in the afternoon. Saw the eclipse on the sun. Mate & I went to the Corners with Shellie, Albert. Came home with Mate. We went up to Wilkinsons.

August, Sunday 8, 1869
Pleasant. After we got our work did, Mate & I went up to Bird's - her nephew came. We went home then down to Uncle Ed's after some ripe apples. Ma & Pa went down to the old Bullard place with Lucy & Vandyne. Mont & Jule came home. Charlie P spent the eve.

The solor corona at eclipse Shelbyville, Kentucky August 7, 1869 by photographer Benjamin Peirce. University of Cambridge, Institute of Astronomy Library.

August, Sunday 8.   1869.

Pleasant - after we got our work did Male & I went up to Birds her nephew came we went home then down to uncle Eds after some ripe apples Ma & I went down to the old Bullard place with Lute & standing there & Julia came home Chastie & spent the

Monday 9.

Pleasant I washed got through by noon then went to bed & stayed till supper time eat my supper went out under the apple tree and sung Jennie saw Borette Abbigail & Earl go past.

Tuesday 10.

Pleasant I ironed all of the fore noon of it Dinner went to bed & slept till supper time after supper went up to Walcox with Aunt Julia met Earl Green I went down to Pete Demello with Lucy & Wes oh dear I am so lonesome

August, Wednesday 11.   1869.

Not very pleasant Aunt Julie & I went a raspberrying got wet through got up to the house and found Vie there practiced all the after noon Earl Green spent the eve

Thursday 12.

Pleasant got up at six oclock eat my breakfast got ready and went up to Mrs Walkers with Vic came home & got Jen & I went down to uncle Eds after some apples came home practiced a little went to bed

Friday 13.

Pleasant had just got my dishes done when Miss Jane Rounds came here stayed all day I went to the creek & to Males came home eat my supper Male & I went out walking Mr Albert stoped and talked a while came home and went to bed

August, Monday 9, 1869
Pleasant. I washed. Got through by noon then went to bed & stayed till supper time. Went out under the apple tree and swung. Jennie saw Rosette, Abbigale & Earl go by.

August, Tuesday 10, 1869
Pleasant. Ironed all of the forenoon. After dinner went to bed & slept till supper time. After supper went up to Mrs. Wilcox with Aunt Julia. Met Earl Green. I went down to Pete Demell's with Lucy & Wes. Oh, dear I am so lonesome.

August, Wednesday 11, 1869
Not very pleasant. Aunt Julia & I went a raspberrying. Got wet through. Got up to the house and found Vic there. Practiced all of the afternoon. Earl Green spent the eve.

August, Thursday 12, 1869
Pleasant. Got up at six o'clock. Eat my breakfast. Got ready and went up to Mr. Walker's with Vic. Came home a-foot. Jen & I went down to Uncle Ed's after some apples. Came home - practiced a little. Jule & I went to bed.

August, Friday 13, 1869
Pleasant. Had just got my dishes done when Mrs. Jane Rounds came here. Stayed all day. I went to the Creek after Mate. Came home. Ate my supper. Mate & I went out walking. Met Albert H stopped and talked a while. Came home and went to bed.

August, Saturday 14, 1869
Pleasant. Went over to Aunt Julia's. Stayed a little while. Came home. Got ready and went to the boat race across the bay in a boat with Albert H & Rosette, Albert & Earl & Mate. Abigale, B--- back about five o'clock. Stayed to Albert's to tea then Earl & I, Mate & Albert took a rig. Albert was drunk. Mate & I did not get home till eleven o'clock.

RES. OF **WM. S. GRIGGS**, HENDERSON, JEFFERSON CO., N.Y.

From *History of Jefferson County, New York*, 1878 page 382C.

RESIDENCE OF GEORGE BUNNEL, HENDERSON, JEFFERSON CO., N.Y.

From *History of Jefferson County, New York*, 1878 page 388B.

August, Sunday 15, 1869
Raining. Mate & I did not get up until eight o'clock. Raining like fun. I went home - ate my breakfast - then Mate & I went down to Uncle Ed's - stayed till three o'clock and set on the steps. Mont was here to see Jule. Earl called her. Pa said I could not go out tonight.

August, Monday 16, 1869
Pleasant. I washed. Did not get through till noon. Vic came at night with Pa.

August, Tuesday 17, 1869
Pleasant. Vic is here. Delia came up here. Stayed a little while. Then I went a piece with her. Sophia Vorce's horse ran a way with here.

August, Wednesday 18, 1869
Pleasant. Practiced two hours.

August, Thursday 19, 1869
Pleasant. Stayed at home until night then Aunt Julia & Elvira & I went to the Village. I stayed all night with Jule. Went down to Moody's to the Sing. Myron W went home with me, Mont with Jule, Earl with Mate.

August, Friday 20, 1869
Pleasant. Did not get up till breakfast was ready. Mrs. Eggleston is not very well this morning. Stayed with Jule all day. Went over to Seatons. Saw Jim. Myron brought me home.

August, Saturday 21, 1869
Raining like fun. Stayed at home all day. Mate down to Vorces. Aunt Julia & I went down to Albert's after some peas. Got home. Aunt Julia gave Mate her blessing and then we went to bed. Jule came home.

August, Sunday 22, 1869
Pleasant. Jule, Everett & I went over to Aunt Lib's. May & John Ray was there. Got home early. Mont and Wes Vandyne had been here. Mont spent the eve and all night. He went back with Pa in the morn.

August, Monday 23, 1869
Pleasant. I washed. Got through by noon. Went over to Aunt Julia's and stayed till supper was ready. Then Mate & I went down to the lake. Came back and set on the hill. Went over to Aunt Julia's and Mate & I sang a song.

August, Tuesday 24, 1869
Pleasant. Jen & I ironed a little. Vic & Addie Walker is here. Mate & I are getting our gloves made for hop picking. Deal come along. I went to the Village with her. Saw Brate Snow. Delia Hallady gave me Charlie Partridge's picture. Got home at eleven o'clock.

August, Wednesday 25, 1869
Pleasant. Went down to Pete's to pick hops. Picked one box. Addie Walker, Aunt Julia, Mate & I are to be -- Noah Ding's boxtenders. Mate & I went up to Rosette's at night. Earl run Mrs. Howard over there. Saw a peddlar.

August, Thursday 26, 1869
Pleasant. Picked hops all day (one box and a half). After tea, Mate & I went up to the graveyard. Took Aunt Julia and some of the other hop pickers home. Saw Albert. Went up to Rogers - turned around - got back to Peter's before they went to bed.

August, Friday 27, 1869
Pleasant. Picked hops all day - box and a half. After tea, Mate & I went up to the school house. Albert & Earl came along. We stayed out so late [that we] had a devil of a time getting into the house - slept four in a bed. Came very near to --- -- my feet.

August, Saturday 28, 1869
Cloudy in the morning. Picked quarter of a box. Commenced to rain. Had to go to the house. Noah took a horse and carried the hop pickers home. 22 in all. Mate is over here tonight.

August, Sunday 29, 1869
Pleasant. Mate & I went out in the weeds to the clearing. Did not get home untill half past four. I ---- Earl & Albert. Saw Brate. Spent the evening over to Mate's. I went to bed at nine.

August, Monday 30, 1869
Pleasant. Picked hops all day. Box and 1/8. Mate & I went up to the road a little way. Came back and went to bed. Slept downstairs.

August, Tuesday 31, 1869
Pleasant. Got up. Went to picking hops - 2 boxes today. Mate and I went up to the shore. Cold enough to win a prize. Got home at bedtime. Slept up in the hall. Mate, Jule, & I. Aunt Eliza come home - baby died.

September, Wednesday 1, 1869
Pleasant. Went to picking hops. Picked 2 boxes. Brate Snow come after. Mate & I went out riding. Mate went with Albert. I with Brate. Got home at ten o'clock.

September, Thursday 2, 1869
Pleasant. Got up and washed the dishes. Got ready and went down to the graveyard. They buried Aunt Eliza's baby and went down to Peter's in the afternoon. Picked one box.

September, Friday 3, 1869
Pleasant. Picked hops - 2 boxes. Mate and I went up to the shore. Got home at bedtime. Slept downstairs.

September, Saturday 4, 1869
Pleasant. Picked hops - one box and three quarters. Got through and all went home. Jule went to the Village. Aunt Eliza came home with her.

September, Sunday 5, 1869
Pleasant. Mate & I went down to Uncle Ed's. Had not been there long when Eliza Sprague & Jeddie came and wanted me to go and pick hops. I went up to Stanley's - Clara, Frank H, & I.

September, Monday 6, 1869
Pleasant. Went to picking hops this morning. Rained a little - just at night. Clara & I slept together. Frank told us stories.

September, Tuesday 7, 1869
Pleasant. Got up to Breakfast. Went out in the hop yard. Picked all day.

Clara & I went down to Jensen's. Herb Bartlett was in the yard today. Frank & Minnie went to the Lodge with him.

September, Wednesday 8, 1869
Pleasant this morn. Picked hops till the middle of the afternoon. Then it commenced to rain. Jeddie & went down to Smithville. Rained like shot all the way there & back.

September, Thursday 9, 1869
Raining. Can't pick hops today. Nettie, Fannie, & Frank, Jeddie & I went up to Mr. Warner's. Frank & I did not get out. Came back and carried Fanny Thompson down to Dar Stanley's.

September, Friday 10, 869
Raining this forenoon but pleasant in the afternoon. Picked hops all the afternoon. Went up to Mr. Hall's and set up with a dead man. George & Ell Bartlet, Jed & I.

September, Saturday 11, 1869
Pleasant. Picked hops all day. Frank & I went with Jed to carry the hop pickers home. Carried Fannie & Marian down to Thompson's. Jed, Chet & I went.

September, Sunday 12, 1869
Pleasant. Frank went home but came back again. I went riding with Herb Barlett. Frank stayed at home. I got home before any of them. Went to bed.

September, Monday 13, 1869
Pleasant. Frank & I got up and went with Jed after the hop pickers. Picked hops all day. Frank, Jed, Chet Ward & I went out cooning at night. Saw Em Crowell today.

September, Tuesday 14, 1869
Pleasant. Frank & I did not get up until all the hop pickers had got there. Picked hops all day. Hop Dance at night. Frank carried Mrs. Washburn home. I went with Jed to carry the rest of them home. Boys all drunk to the Hop Dance.

September, Wednesday 15, 1869
Pleasant. Frank & I got up at daylight. Frank went up after Mrs. Washburn & I went with Jeddie after the other hop pickers. Picked hops all the forenoon. I carried Mrs. Luce home, then Frank & I went in the hop yard with Jed after he came home at night.

September, Thursday 16, 1869
Pleasant. Got up to breakfast. Did the work. Ell Vorce & Deal Howard came along for Mate & I to go down to Gleasons. Went a-foot. Did not get home till dark.

September, Friday 17, 1869
Pleasant. Stayed at home. Saw Albert Hungerford go down. Mate & I went down after some apples at night.

September, Saturday 18, 1869
Pleasant. Did not get up till breakfast was ready. Got dinner & supper. Went to the Corners with Elvira & Mate. Earl past [passed] us. Saw Earl driving a cutter by here today.

September, Sunday 19, 1869
Pleasant. Got breakfast. Did all the work. Ma & Pa went up to Vandynes. Have not got home yet. Saw Jim Seaton go past.

End of diary

September, Monday 13. 1869.

Pleasant Frank & I got up
and went with Jed after
the hop pickers picked hops
all day Frank Jed Chet
Hazel & I went out coasting
at night ran & in owing
to day

Tuesday 14.

Pleasant Frank & I did not
get up untill all the hop pickers
had got there, picked hops
all day hop dance at night
Frank carried Mrs Hashler home
I went with Jed to carrie the
rest of them home boys all
drunk to the hop dance

Wednesday 15.

Pleasant Frank & I got
up at daylight. Frank
went up after Mrs Thrash
& I went with J, & in
after the other hop pickers
picked hops all the fore
noon I carried Mrs Lucas
home then Frank & I went
in the hop land our Jed
the hop dance at night

September, Thursday 16. 1869.

Pleasant got up to
breakfast did the work
Ett Price & Deal Howard
came along for Mate
& I to go down to Glass
Glass's went along
did not get home till
dark

Friday 17.

Pleasant stayed at
home all day ran
Ellert & Sam got over
go down, Mate & I
went down after some
apples at night

Saturday 18.

Pleasant did not get up
till breakfast was ready
got dinner & supper
went to the corner
with Elvira & Mate
Earl past us, ran
Earl driving a critter
by here to day

Written in the back of the diary

January 28, 1872
Florence White & Myron Whitney were married

She kept a list of invitations

Hallidays with Wort Whitney
Luces with Charlie Howard
Hoveys - Monroe Ray
Juds with Charlie H
Lodge with Charlie H
French Dance with Charlie H - did not accept
Rays Party - Albert Hungerford
Riding - Charlie Howard
Halliday's Dance - Charlie Howard.
Festival to Halladays with Albert
Lucy Vandyne's with Albert
Barneys with Wort W.
Champlins with Charlie Howard - could not go
Albert W with Shelly R to the Lodge Charlie H but could not go
Warner with Wort
Whitney - riding Brate Snow
Riding Jennie Lovell
Vorces - Albert Hungerford
Moodys - Will Crittenden - did not accept

June 13
Jule bet I would get married first - if I do not she has got to give me 5 dollars - If I do I am to give her the same

Dear Phebe,

Tonight I am going away & maybe will not see you in a long time & maybe never, but bear in mind I love you better than any one in this world and always shall no matter what happens to us in our after life. I love you dearly. When you read this I shall be far away, but think often of the one who loves you better than her own life -- know I mean what I say. Never show anybody this, they might think it silly.

Good bye my best & dearest
Florence

I shall always remember my promise to you.

Number of Beaus [and what time she got home]

Date	Name	Time
Jan 10	Charlie Howard	12 o'clock
Jan 8	Harlie Howard	9 o'clock
Jan 24	Wort Whitney	scratched out
Jan 28	Leslie Boyce	9 o'clock
Jan 30	Ed Howard	12 o'clock
Jan 30	Wort Whitney	10 o'clock
Jan 31	Arthur Kilby	11:30 o'clock
Feb 3	Harlie & Leslie	12 o'clock
Feb 4	Charlie Howard	12 o'clock
Feb 14	Brate Snow	1 o'clock
Feb 21	Wort Whitney	12 o'clock
Feb 28	Jim Seaton	9 o'clock
March 2	Harlie & Leslie	12 o'clock
March 11	David Montague	12:30 o'clock
March 14	Brate Snow	11 o'clock
March 21	Brate Snow	10 o'clock
March 24	Frank Whitney	11:30 o'clock
March 31	D M	10 o'clock
April 2	Harlie H & Charlie & D M	2 o'clock
April 3	Harlie & Leslie	12 o'clock
April 11	David Montague	12 o'clock
April 25	Brate Snow	12 o'clock
May 16	Wort Whitney	10 o'clock
May 28	Ernie Chapman	10 o'clock
May 30	Brate Snow	12 o'clock
July 15	Shelly Rounds	12 o'clock
July 18	Earl Green	1 o'clock
July 21	Charlie Partridge	12 o'clock
July 25	Charlie Partridge	1 o'clock
July 28	Charlie Partridge	12 o'clock
Aug 1	Charlie Partridge	1 o'clock
Aug 5	Charlie Partridge	12 o'clock
Aug 8	Charlie Partridge	2 o'clock
Aug 11	Earl Green	11 o'clock

1866
April 15. Bet
Florence 25¢ that Oliver Gill & Jule White would be married in two years from that day and I bet 25¢ that they wouldn't. The bet was decided 1868. I won. She had a year to pay me but did not so she will commence paying interest 2 cents. April 15, 1869.

Signed
27 March 1869
Florence White
Jennie White
Phebe White

Phebe White
Florence and I made another bet on 1 January 1868. I bet 25 cents that Ernie Chapman would marry Em Snow. She bet 25 cents he would not. If they marry each other she is to give me 25 cents, if not I give her 25 cents. In the meantime, if they marry someone else and if Ernie's wife dies and Em's husband dies and then they marry each other she is to pay me back 25 cents.

Signed 27 March 1868
Florence White
Jennie White
Phebe White

Spring Cake
Brake two eggs in a cup & fill it up with sweet cream. One cup of sugar & one of flour, one teaspoon of cream of tartar, half teaspoon of saleratus.

List of Students that went to Belleville Fall Term 1870
Agnes Randell
--- Wallace
Anna Cooper
Addlie Graves
Alice Waterbury
Carrie Chapman
Carrie Fillmore
Clara Garver
Carrie R--
Eva Wood
Eva Hawley
Eve Stanley
Evy Tracy
Evy Graves
Em Graves
Em --sley
Em Clark
Eve Graves
Em Reynolds
Elln Webb
Ell vorce
Dorg Williams
Delia Garvis

Sponge Cake
three eggs, cup of sugar, half cup sweet milk, one teaspoon cream of tartar, half teaspoon of soda, cup of flour

White Cake
whites of three eggs, half cup of sweet cream, teaspoon of cream of tartar, half teaspoon of soda, cup of flour

Jelly Cake
one cup of sugar, 2/3 cup sweet milk, 1 teaspoon cream of tartar, half teaspoon saleratus, 1 egg, three table spoons melted butter, half

Phebe White Partridge is buried in the Hungerford Cemetery in Henderson, New York. Her stone erroneously says she died at the age of 22, it should be 26. Photo courtesy of NNYGenealogy www.nnygenealogy.com

Afterward

Phebe briefly taught school in nearby Belleville, New York in 1869 and 1870. She married her beau Charlie Partridge and they moved to the West. She died eight years after the last entry in this diary.

A newspaper account of her death reads, "The remains of Phebe, wife of Mr. Chas. Partridge, and daughter of Captain James M. White, of Henderson, were last week conveyed through this place, from the West, to be interred near the home of her childhood in Henderson." She had no children.

Bibliography

From *Gazetteer and directory of Jefferson County, New York*, for 1866-7 Watertown, N.Y.: I Ingalls & Co., Printer and Bookbinders, 1866, Child, Hamilton.

Haddock, John A. *The growth of a century: as illustrated in the history of Jefferson county, New York, from 1793 to 1894*. Philadelphia: Sherman & Co., 1894.

History of Jefferson County, New York 1797-1878. Philadelphia: L.H. Everts, 1878.

Jefferson County Journal, Adams, NY December 25, 1873.

Jefferson County Journal, Adams, NY June 14, 1914.

Jefferson County Journal, Adams, NY May 9, 1911.

Jefferson County Journal, Adams, NY March 12, 1924.

Special thanks to

Elaine Scott, Henderson Historical Society
Debbie Quick, Historical Association of South Jefferson
Sid & Bonnie, NNYGenealogy

More *Learning From History* publications from
New York History Review Press

Plank Road Explorer
by Henry Marvin, 1873-1874

A Darned Good Time
by Miss Lucy Potter, 1868

My Centennial Diary - A Year in the Life of a Country Boy by Earll K. Gurnee, 1876

My Story - A Year in the Life of a Country Girl
by Ida Burnett, 1880

Queen City Adventure
by Emma Latier, 1902

Home In These Hills
Viola Coolbaugh, 1891

www.ingramcontent.com/pod-product-compliance
Lightning Source LLC
Chambersburg PA
CBHW051713040426
42446CB00008B/867